Animals
NEAR
and
FAR

amicus
readers

Mankato, Minnesota

by Jenna Lee Gleisner

Ideas for Parents and Teachers

Amicus Readers let children practice reading informational texts at the earliest reading levels. Familiar words and concepts with close photo-text matches support early readers.

Before Reading
- Discuss the cover photo with the child. What does it tell him?
- Ask the child to predict what she will learn in the book.

Read the Book
- "Walk" through the book and look at the photos. Let the child ask questions.
- Read the book to the child, or have the child read independently.

After Reading
- Use the photo quiz at the end of the book to review the text.
- Prompt the child to make connections. Ask: *What animals are near or far from you?*

Amicus Readers are published by Amicus
P.O. Box 1329, Mankato, MN 56002
www.amicuspublishing.us

Library of Congress Cataloging-in-Publication Data

Gleisner, Jenna Lee.
  Animals near and far / Jenna Lee Gleisner.
    pages cm. -- (Animal Antonyms)
  ISBN 978-1-60753-504-1 (hardcover) -- ISBN 978-1-60753-533-1 (eBook)
1. English language--Synonyms and antonyms--Juvenile literature. 2. English language--Comparison--Juvenile literature. 3. Animals--Juvenile literature. I. Title.
  PE1591.G556 2013
  428.1--dc23
                    2013010412

Photo Credits: Shutterstock Images, cover (top), 3 (top), 5, 10, 12, 14, 16 (top middle), 16 (top right); Nickolay Stanev/Shutterstock Images, cover (bottom); Thinkstock, 1 (top front), 1 (top back); Gary C. Tognoni/Shutterstock Images, 1 (bottom); Oleg Znamenskiy/Shutterstock Images, 3 (bottom), 16 (top left); Vladimir Chernyanskiy/Shutterstock Images, 4; Maggy Meyer/Shutterstock Images, 6; J Reineke/Shutterstock Images, 7; Arnon Polin/Shutterstock Images, 8, 16 (bottom middle); Lawrence Cruciana/Shutterstock Images, 9; Serg Zastavkin/Shutterstock Images, 11; Wendy Nero/Shutterstock Images, 13 (16 (bottom right); Armin Rose/Shutterstock Images, 15, 16 (bottom left)

Produced for Amicus by The Peterson Publishing Company and Red Line Editorial.

Editor Jenna Gleisner
Designer Jake Nordby
Printed in the United States of America
Mankato, MN
July, 2013
PA 1938
10 9 8 7 6 5 4 3 2 1

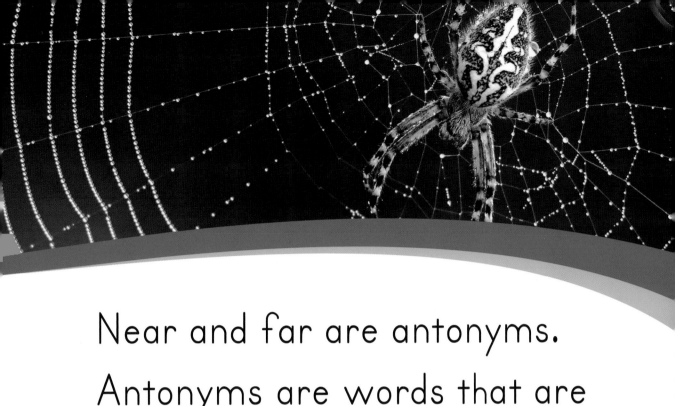

Near and far are antonyms. Antonyms are words that are opposites. Are there animals near you?

Fox pups stay near
their dens. Here, they
stay safe.

Butterflies fly far south in the winter. There, they can stay warm.

Lions sneak up near their prey.

Zebras run far away
from lions.

Seahorses hide near
coral to stay safe.

Sharks are safe in the open ocean. Some swim far to look for food.

Spiders stay near their
webs. They wait for
insects to get stuck.

Some beetles travel
far across the desert
to find food.

Honey bees work near each other to make honey. Their group is called a colony.

Far away, a black bear hunts for food alone.

Father penguins huddle
near each other to keep
warm.

14

Mother penguins swim
far away. They will come
home with food for their
babies.

Photo Quiz

Which animals are near?
Which animals are far?